Information Systems Engineering Library

Database Language SQL Explained

CCTA

September 1993

LONDON: HMSO

© Crown Copyright 1993

Applications for reproduction should be made to HMSO

First published 1993

ISBN 0 11 330583 4
ISSN 0967-9561

For further information regarding this publication and other CCTA products please contact:

CCTA Library
Riverwalk House
157-161 Millbank
London SW7P 4RT

071-217-3331

Contents

Foreword

1 **Introduction**   1

    1.1   Purpose of this volume

    1.2   Who should read this volume

    1.3   Structure of this volume

    1.4   Terminology

2 **Overview: summary of key messages**   5

    2.1   What is SQL?

    2.2   Why use SQL?

    2.3   SQL-92

    2.4   Publicly available specifications

    2.5   Availability of conforming products

    2.6   SQL conformance claims

    2.7   SQL conformance testing

    2.8   Procurements involving SQL

    2.9   Reserved keywords

    2.10   Future development

3 Introduction to SQL — 9

- 3.1 Business context of IS
- 3.2 Challenges facing IT
- 3.3 Role of open systems
- 3.4 Overview of SQL
- 3.5 Benefits of SQL

4 Technical context of SQL — 21

- 4.1 Related technologies
- 4.2 Standards context of SQL

5 International standard for SQL — 31

- 5.1 SQL standards process
- 5.2 Evolution of the standard
- 5.3 Scope of SQL-92
- 5.4 SQL-92 conformance levels
- 5.5 Major new facilities in SQL-92

6 Related standardisation activities — 39

- 6.1 SQL-supporting international standards
- 6.2 Consortia standardisation bodies

7 Conformance and timescales   45

     7.1   Conformance testing and vendor claims

     7.2   SQL-92 conformance claims and testing

     7.3   RDA conformance testing

     7.4   Timescales for SQL-92

     7.5   Timescales for RDA

8 SQL, RDA and procurements   49

     8.1   Procurements involving SQL

     8.2   Procurements involving RDA

9 Future developments of SQL   53

     9.1   SQL3 facilities

     9.2   Timescales for SQL3

Annexes

A SQL standards documents   57

     A.1   International standard

     A.2   National standards

     A.3   Vendor specifications

     A.4   FIPS PUBS

B SQL-92 facilities   61

     B.1   Entry SQL-92

     B.2   Intermediate SQL-92

     B.3   Full SQL-92

C	**Migrating applications from SQL-89 to SQL-92**	**71**
	C.1 Compatibility of Entry SQL-92 with SQL-89	
	C.2 Migration	
D	**New reserved keywords**	**73**
	Bibliography	**75**
	Glossary	**79**
	Index	**85**

Foreword

The **Information Systems Engineering Library** provides guidance on managing and carrying out Information Systems Engineering activities. In the IS life cycle, Information Systems Engineering takes place once the IS strategy has been defined. It is concerned with the development and ongoing improvement of information systems up to the operational stage, when systems become the responsibility of infrastructure management.

The Information Systems Engineering Library builds on guidance in the CCTA IS Guides, particularly set A: *Management and Planning Set* and set B: *Systems Development Set* and complements other CCTA products, in particular the project management method, PRINCE, and the systems analysis and design method, SSADM.

Volumes in the Information Systems Engineering Library are of interest to varying levels of staff from IS directors to IS providers, helping them to improve the quality and productivity of their IS development work. Some volumes in this library should also be of interest to business managers, IS user's and those involved in market testing, whose business operations depend on having effective IS support by means of Information Systems Engineering activities.

The Information Systems Engineering Library also complements other related CCTA publications, particularly the IT Infrastructure Library for operational issues and the IS Planning Subject Guides for strategic issues.

CCTA welcomes customer views on Information Systems Engineering Library publications. Please send your comments to:

Customer Services
Information Systems Engineering Group
Gildengate House
Upper Green Lane
NORWICH
NR3 1DW

Acknowledgements

CCTA wishes to gratefully acknowledge the assistance of the following organisations in the preparation of this volume:

Edinburgh University
Hoskyns Group plc

Valuable contributions were also made by:

Directorate of Health Services in Scotland
NHS Information Management Centre
NCC
NIST

1 Introduction

1.1 Purpose of this volume

The purpose of this volume is to:

- show the contribution SQL can make to putting an IS strategy into practice and thus to achieving business objectives, when it is adopted as part of technical policies for open systems and data management

- describe the relationship of the current international standard for SQL, SQL-92 (see section 1.4), with related standards

- outline the main features of SQL-92

- explain when, where and how SQL-92 can be used in procurement

- outline how the international standard for SQL is likely to evolve in the future.

This volume is not intended as a tutorial on either the SQL language or specific products. Such information may be found in generally available text books (see the bibliography) and in vendor documentation.

1.2 Who should read this volume

This volume is primarily aimed at IT technical planners involved in defining technical policies for standards and architectures. Project teams involved in planning, obtaining or implementing relational database systems should read chapters 7 and 8 in particular.

This volume will also be of interest to application programmers, specifically Annex D.

1.3 Structure of this volume

Chapter 2 summarises the key messages contained in this volume.

Chapter 3 sets the business context for SQL by describing the business and IT challenges facing organisations, and the approaches being taken to address them. It then introduces SQL and describes its applicability and benefits. It will be useful to planners deciding whether SQL is a suitable data management standard for their organisations' application areas.

Chapter 4 discusses technologies with which SQL may be used and others against which it may compete, before describing its relationship with other IT standards.

Chapter 5 describes the new international standard in terms of its development, its conformance levels and its new facilities. Descriptions of the new facilities will be of particular interest to planners whilst details of conformance levels will be useful to staff communicating with suppliers either in the context of procurements or when making general enquiries about product developments.

Chapter 6 outlines various standards that either directly reference SQL or are designed to support an SQL environment. These standards are likely to be referenced by software suppliers and so will be of interest to staff having to communicate with software vendors. This chapter does not reference or describe standards which may be used in conjunction with SQL unless they explicitly refer to SQL.

Chapter 7 provides an indication of when SQL facilities are likely to be available. It also describes conformance testing and defines the attributes to be checked when a vendor claims conformance to a standard. It will be of particular interest to those involved in procurements.

Chapter 8 provides guidelines for those procuring SQL-conforming products. As future SQL-application procurements may involve limited distribution of data, guidelines on Remote Database Access (RDA) are also included.

Chapter 9 identifies the major facilities likely to be included in any future development of SQL. This information is provided for long range planning purposes.

Annex A lists the various SQL standards documents and notes minor differences between these documents.

Annex B outlines the new facilities included in SQL-92 and is based on the list of proposals accepted during the standard's development. It will therefore be necessary to consult the standard itself where a detailed understanding of these facilities is required.

Annex C lists the minor incompatibilities between SQL-92 and the previous SQL standard, and describes how applications conforming to the previous SQL standard can be migrated to SQL-92 environments.

Annex D lists the new reserved keywords introduced in SQL-92. These should be brought to the attention of application programmers since applications which use these new keywords as identifiers require modification before they can be migrated to products conforming to SQL-92.

1.4 Terminology

Throughout the remainder of this volume, references to SQL-92 are to be interpreted as allusions to the SQL language as defined in the international standard ISO/IEC 9075:1992 *Database Language SQL*. This revision of the standard has been referred to in the computer press and other publications as *SQL2*. References to SQL-89 are to be interpreted as allusions to the now superseded international standard ISO/IEC 9075:1989. SQL-87 and SQL-89 are often referred to as *SQL-1* and *SQL-1 with addendum* respectively. References to *SQL3* allude to the anticipated revision of the SQL-92 standard.

References to *RDA* allude to the international standards 9579-1: *Remote Database Access - Part 1, Generic model, service and protocol* and 9579-2: *Remote Database Access - Part 2, SQL specialisation*, which were approved and published as international standards late in 1992.

2 Overview: summary of key messages

2.1 What is SQL?

SQL, pronounced SEQUEL and an abbreviation for Structured Query Language, was originally a language for the access, manipulation and querying of data in relational databases. It now has a much broader role and its international standard gives it the title, 'Database Language SQL', to reflect this broader role.

2.2 Why use SQL?

Most organisations introduce technical policies such as open systems and data management to ensure that a common approach is adopted across all business areas. SQL has an important role to play in putting these technical policies into practice.

SQL is the industry accepted interface between applications and relational databases and is increasingly used to access non-relational data. It is therefore an important tool in achieving data integration across different databases.

Since SQL provides a standard target environment for application software, its use can facilitate the portability of applications between different vendor environments.

SQL is used by software developers because it provides increased productivity and more flexible query functionality. SQL is also generated automatically by fourth generation languages (4GLs) and end user packages that provide simple access to data.

SQL, together with the standard for Remote Database Access (RDA), can provide a standard way of accessing data stored on remote databases.

The European Council IT Standards Decision 87/95/EEC requires member states to ensure that references are made to European standards or prestandards, or international standards, in public procurement orders exceeding a value of 100,000 ECU relating to information technology.

This Decision applies to standards used as the basis for the exchange of information and data for systems interoperability. The Decision is not restricted to central government. Other public sector bodies covered by the Decision include local government, education, police and fire authorities, new town corporations and EEC funded bodies. Failure to comply with this Decision could lead to challenge and halted procurements.

2.3 SQL-92

An international standard for SQL has existed since 1987 and a new version of this standard, commonly referred to as SQL-92, has recently been released.

SQL-92 replaces SQL-89 and includes significant new functionality. The language defined by SQL-92 is generally upward compatible with that defined by earlier versions of the SQL standard.

SQL-92 specifies three conformance levels: Entry, Intermediate and Full and three binding styles: module, embedded and direct. SQL-92 supports seven standard host programming languages: Ada, C, COBOL, FORTRAN, MUMPS, Pascal and PL/I.

2.4 Publicly available specifications

Vendor consortia such as the SQL-Access Group and X/Open publish industry-agreed SQL specifications. These specifications are generally compatible with national and international standards but usually represent a subset of their functionality.

2.5 Availability of conforming products

Vendors are likely to implement facilities compatible with the SQL-92 standard incrementally. For example, SQL with RDA, providing limited client-server operation in an open systems environment, is likely to be available from a number of vendors by 1994. Products conforming to Full SQL-92 are likely to be available by the mid 1990s.

Chapter 2
Overview: summary of key messages

2.6	SQL conformance claims	Vendors' claims of conformance to SQL-92 should specify the conformance level, the binding styles and the host programming languages supported by their products.
2.7	SQL conformance testing	A software vendor's products must have passed a recognised set of conformance tests to legitimately claim conformance to a recognised standard.

In the case of SQL, successfully fulfilling the requirements of a conformance test implies correct processing of SQL statements according to the syntactic and semantic rules defined in the standard. It implies no guarantees about the product's performance or capacity.

Currently the only SQL conformance testing available is undertaken by the National Institute of Standards and Technology in the USA, who maintain a list of conforming products. At present, the tests check for conformance to SQL-89 but it is expected that conformance testing for Entry SQL-92 will be available by mid 1993.

Conformance tests for SQL with RDA are unlikely to be available until 1995.

2.8	Procurements involving SQL	From 1 January 1994, government organisations procuring SQL-based databases or related products should require, as a minimum, that products conform to Entry SQL-92 (ISO 9075:1992).

In circumstances where IS planners and purchasers decide that the XPG4 CAE Specification for SQL provides a solution or migration path that better meets the immediate needs of an individual project, compliance with the CAE Specification should be specified as highly desirable. In order to comply with the EC public procurement legislation this requirement should not be made mandatory, unless a valid overriding technical or economic case for doing so can be established.

Further, government organisations should be aware that, because the CAE specification places additional requirements on the supplier, the differences between SQL-92 and the CAE Specification could cause compatibility problems.

Until 31 December 1993, government organisations should continue to require conformance to SQL-89.

2.9 Reserved keywords

Application programmers should avoid using keywords as identifiers within applications. Applications using reserved keywords as identifiers are not *standard-conforming programs* and may require modification before they can be successfully migrated to a product conforming to the SQL-92 standard.

2.10 Future development

A further enhancement of the international SQL standard is under development. This version, often referred to as SQL3, is unlikely to be available before the mid 1990s.

3 Introduction to SQL

In order to set SQL in a business context, this chapter:

- discusses a number of business challenges facing organisations and the approaches being taken to address them (see section 3.1)

- outlines the challenges facing IT and some of the technical approaches which are being used to meet them (see section 3.2)

- outlines the role of open systems (see section 3.3).

This is followed by an introduction to SQL which:

- provides an overview of SQL describing how and where it is used (see section 3.4)

- discusses the benefits of using SQL (see section 3.5).

3.1 Business context of IS

Public and private sector organisations are trying to improve their effectiveness and efficiency, and the quality of service they offer their customers. Government organisations face the challenge of making the best possible use of public money in the face of market testing and increasing demand for services. Businesses must respond to the demands of the European Single Market and an increasingly global marketplace.

3.1.1 Business approach

There are many broad categories of business approaches that address these challenges, including:

- reduced costs

    Government organisations must often provide more services without increasing their demands on public funds, while businesses must compete with new low-cost suppliers

- empowerment

    This aims to devolve decision-making responsibilities as far down the management chain as possible, so that those who make the product or deliver the service can make on-the-spot decisions without the delay involved in getting approval from supervisors or managers. The objective is to improve quality as perceived by the customer. The technical challenge is for information systems to provide the required information immediately to whoever requires it

- customer-centred service

    Customers expect easier dealings with organisations. This may require the drawing together of the service organisation and the supporting information systems so that customer contacts can be handled with all necessary transactions, more conveniently for the customer. For example, a customer should not have to repeat the same information to several different members of an organisation simply to make a number of different requests

- faster time-to-market

    As competition increases, it becomes crucial to speed the introduction of new products and services. The technical challenge is to deliver information systems that support these innovations. For example, government organisations may be required to collect and process new information to cope with UK and European legislation; changes often have to be introduced within very tight timescales. Manufacturing companies frequently look towards 'concurrent engineering', in which a team involving design, production, marketing and other people work together to drastically reduce time-to-market for new products

- database marketing

  This aims to use information collected about customers, including purchase history, to define market requirements for new products and services, and generate increased sales. A common example is cross-selling, which aims to sell products or services that are complementary to those already bought by a given customer

- continuous quality improvement

  Customer satisfaction is highly dependent on the perceived quality of products and services. Continually improving quality is therefore essential to many businesses.

3.2 Challenges facing IT

All these approaches make significant demands on IT, including:

- quicker delivery time for applications which support the business approaches adopted and at a lower cost

- use of lower cost platforms enabling either more users to be supported or cost reductions to be achieved

- integration of data from diverse systems

- provision of new types of application based on technological developments such as imaging.

3.2.1 Technical approach

The technical approaches that are being used to meet these demands include:

- developing new applications on, or migrating existing applications to, the most appropriately sized platform: *rightsizing*.

Rightsizing can provide a number of advantages, including lower platform costs and more productive development tools. It is sometimes known as *downsizing*, but the term rightsizing is generally preferred since it does not assume that movement is always from larger to smaller platforms

- deploying new technology

- providing a manageable technical architecture that supports all the above, together with a consistent user interface and the capability to support new application areas such as document imaging. In this context, technical architecture is the set of all interfaces, whether de jure standards or de facto specifications, and products conforming to those interfaces, which meet an organisation's IT requirements.

3.3 Role of open systems

While all the technical approaches in section 3.2.1 are possible with a mix of different platforms from different vendors, the most efficient way of making these approaches work is to have a policy of using open systems. This involves selecting appropriate de jure standards, together with de facto specifications where de jure standards are not yet available in products, and integrating them into a technical architecture that provides the following attributes:

- application and data portability across platforms either from different vendors or which use different technologies. This allows a free choice of the most appropriate vendor platform; different technologies, for example, reduced instruction set computer (RISC), can be incorporated as appropriate

- inter-operability, which is the ability to exchange data and invoke functions regardless of application and platform boundaries and without difficulties in interfacing applications or platforms from different vendors. Like portability, this allows a free choice of platform while simplifying the use of multiple applications.

In addition, the use of open systems means that users and developers need only acquire a single set of platform-independent skills for their respective areas, such as the user interface or development environment. This portability of skills supports the free choice of platforms and improves staff flexibility.

3.3.1 Benefits of open systems

These attributes of open systems architectures provide a number of benefits including:

- reduced cost of platforms in the longer term, since there will be fewer technical constraints on platform selection, thus allowing their procurement in a highly competitive market as commodity items

- reduced cost of application and system software, since all platforms conforming to the same standards will allow software developers to target a large single market

- increased staff flexibility. Developers need learn only one set of technical skills to be able to develop for any platform, whilst users can utilise applications running on different platforms more easily, because the user interface style is consistent

- protection of investment in applications and platforms as new technology can be incorporated whilst rendering fewer applications obsolete

- easier integration of existing data and functions from diverse information systems as a result of inter-operability

- vendor independence. If a vendor runs into difficulties that impinge on its ability to provide support to develop new products, the business is faced with unexpectedly moving to another platform. However, open systems lessen the likelihood that re-development will be highly costly and time consuming.

For some organisations, the use of standards is not simply a matter of obtaining benefits. The European Council IT Standards Decision 87/95/EEC requires member states to ensure that references are made where appropriate to European standards or prestandards, or international standards, in public procurement orders exceeding a value of 100,000 ECU relating to information technology.

Open systems may involve increased costs for services such as systems integration, training and data management.

3.4 Overview of SQL

As a prelude to examining the benefits of SQL in contributing an 'IT response' to an organisation's business needs, it is necessary to describe what SQL is and what it does.

SQL is the industry accepted interface between applications and relational databases and is increasingly used to access non-relational data. It is therefore an important tool in achieving data integration.

In practice, SQL is primarily used by software developers with fourth generation languages (4GLs) or with third generation languages (3GLs) such as COBOL. Whichever type of language is used, SQL can contribute to increased productivity by simplifying the provision of flexible query functionality to the user. SQL is also generated automatically by 4GLs and end user packages that provide simple access to data, without the delays and costs of requiring special software to be developed for each query.

3.4.1 Applicability of SQL

SQL is a suitable language for applications requiring to store and manipulate data that can be represented as tables.

Generally, implementations of SQL are targeted towards supporting larger, multi-user applications based on mainframes, mini-computers or large workstations. Such products can be expected to include recovery, concurrency control and security features necessary for multi-user applications. However, some implementations of SQL operate on single-user microcomputers or PCs.

While SQL databases can include fields that contain textual data, the SQL language is not generally suited for *free text information retrieval* applications. These applications need to search large volumes of textual data for the existence of specific words or phrases. Such applications are generally better served by employing specialist *free text* data management software rather than relational database software.

SQL may be used in distributed environments where users can, via a workstation or an SQL-client, access data located on one or more SQL-servers. Such distributed architectures can, by employing suitable underlying communications capabilities such as those provided by Remote Database Access (RDA), be open systems, involving clients and SQL-servers from different software vendors.

3.4.2 SQL and RDA standards

An international standard for SQL has existed since 1987 and a new version of this standard, commonly referred to as SQL-92, has recently been published.

Remote Database Access (RDA), a recently completed international standard, can be used with SQL to specify how an SQL application located on one platform interacts with an SQL implementation located on another.

Using SQL and RDA standards can lead to reduced costs as a result of open systems benefits such as:

- portability of applications and data between platforms from different vendors or using different types of database

- the ability of any SQL application to use any SQL database.

In the rest of this chapter, the use of SQL is assumed to include the use of RDA to provide inter-operability.

3.5 Benefits of SQL

Successfully addressing the business issues outlined in section 3.1 is dependent, in part, on implementing the technical approaches outlined in sections 3.2 and 3.3, particularly the use of open systems. The business benefits of using SQL hinge on its support for these technical approaches.

SQL supports all the technical approaches discussed:

- SQL is used in rightsizing since it is the only common standard for data management on mainframes and on platforms such as UNIX and PC LANs, which are frequently used for rightsizing. The development tools which run on these platforms, such as 4GLs which automatically generate SQL, are typically more productive than traditional development tools, such as COBOL, although the latter has the advantage of being a standard

- SQL has perhaps its greatest impact on data integration across rightsized and legacy systems. In a typical scenario, an application runs as a client on a rightsized system, accessing data from SQL database servers running on either rightsized or legacy systems (see Figure 1).

Where the SQL database server is relational, there are few problems with integration as SQL is directly supported by relational databases on both rightsized and legacy platforms.

However, SQL is increasingly used as an interface to non-relational, legacy data formats such as Indexed Sequential Access Method (ISAM) files, hierarchical databases and network model (CODASYL) databases. Although SQL interfaces to these formats are often limited and the use of SQL to update unnormalised, non-relational data can compromise data integrity, such SQL interfaces, when correctly used, can significantly ease the problem of data integration

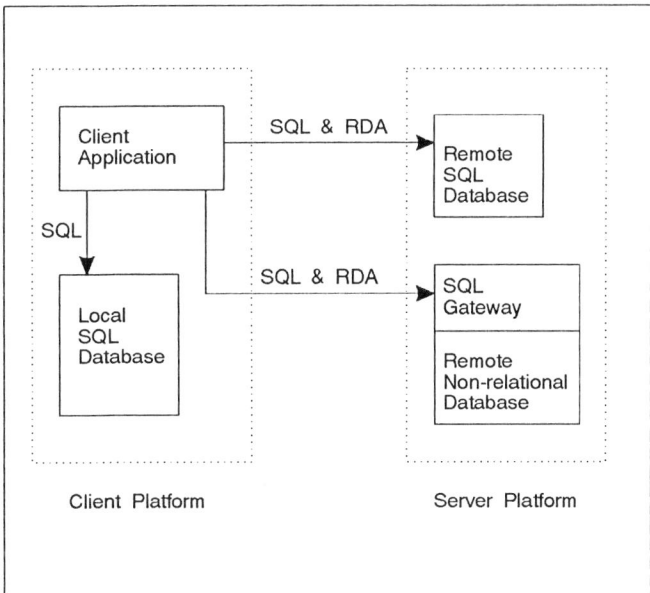

Figure 1:   *Achieving database integration with SQL and RDA*

- SQL is a 'lingua franca' for data integration, enabling developers and users to concentrate on reconciling and integrating data rather than on the mechanics of data access. Using SQL to integrate disparate databases is superior to the common approach of writing a data extraction program to generate a file that is then transferred across the network to the rightsized system, where it is loaded. SQL provides timely access to data at much lower cost in developer and user effort

- SQL is a key component of the technical policies associated with many organisations' IS strategies. Some SQL implementations also provide non-standard support for new application areas such as document imaging, by enabling image storage and access through the SQL interface.

SQL is also relevant in implementing an open systems policy. In addition to the international standards, publicly available specifications have been developed for SQL and RDA which aim to improve portability and inter-operability. These publicly available specifications are:

- X/Open's CAE specification for SQL which is based on SQL-92

- X/Open's preliminary specification for SQL Remote Database Access which is based on the international standard for RDA and work by the SQL-Access Group.

While these standards are independent of a single vendor, there are also some vendor-controlled de facto standards. These may be useful in specific circumstances but are less compatible with an open systems policy.

Chapter 3
Introduction to SQL

Use of the international standards for SQL and RDA, and optionally the publicly available specifications, is assumed here, since this will help to ensure that the benefits of open systems are achieved. In particular, the following technical benefits result from the use of the standards:

- SQL contributes to application and data portability, since SQL is a major part of application source code and is relatively portable, even if the application is written in a non-standard language, such as a 4GL. In general, data portability between SQL databases can be achieved fairly easily, since the relational model maps straightforwardly onto the flat files used for transfer and the basic data types are quite consistent between SQL implementations

- SQL and SQL implementations are scalable:

    - SQL-servers can run on virtually any platform, from desktop PCs, for personal applications, to mainframes, for large transaction processing workloads

    - SQL-clients can run on any platform from mainframes down to radio-connected palmtop PCs

- SQL enhances inter-operability between multiple applications provided that they use SQL to access their data. The applications may be on different platforms and may perform very different functions. SQL also enhances inter-operability between different vendors' platforms, since a SQL-client application can access a SQL-server regardless of the platform on which each is running

- SQL has no direct impact on the user interface and does not conflict with a requirement for consistency.

In delivering these technical benefits of open systems architectures, SQL provides a number of business benefits:

- access to lower cost platforms, and potentially to lower cost SQL-servers, since the existence of the standard interface is leading to SQL database servers becoming a commodity

- access to new technology, although generally new technology has to be accessed via non-standard parts of the SQL interface. For example, document imaging is available using SQL, while some object oriented databases already provide an SQL interface

- vendor independence. SQL can provide independence of both platform and SQL server vendor, thus avoiding costly redevelopments when changing vendors

- increased availability of software packages. Many packages are written to use SQL databases and some of these work with multiple SQL servers

- increased staff flexibility for developers. Once trained in SQL, conversion to use a different SQL server is straightforward

- increased operational flexibility. This is provided through SQL's support for scalability.

In addition, use of SQL should result in faster and easier development of applications, in particular those with complex query and update requirements.

In summary, SQL is highly relevant to the IT challenges of today and thereby helps to address some of the business challenges facing all kinds of organisations.

4 Technical context of SQL

This chapter:

- discusses technological developments related to SQL (see section 4.1)

- positions SQL in relation to other international standards, publicly available specifications and de facto standards (see section 4.2).

4.1 Related technologies

Relational database technology is useful but is not a panacea. While SQL is now the industry accepted applications interface to relational databases, there are many other technologies with which SQL can be used and against which SQL may compete in the future. This section looks at the most important of these technologies.

4.1.1 CASE and 4GLs

Computer Aided Software Engineering (CASE) tools and 4GL tools are increasingly used with SQL databases. Many CASE tools generate table definitions using SQL, but few generate SQL statements for retrievals and updates. Many 4GLs have much closer links to SQL than do CASE tools. Some hide the use of SQL from the developer, generating all required SQL statements, while many provide full access to SQL within the 4GL itself.

4.1.2 Client/server computing

Client/server computing involves structuring application and system software into clients and servers. Client software, which interfaces directly with the user, typically runs on a dedicated desktop workstation, such as a PC, and makes requests of server software, which runs on a platform that provides larger data storage capacity and access to shared resources, such as printers.

SQL was not designed for client/server computing but it can be used for many types of client/server system. The SQL interface becomes the client/server interface between SQL client applications and SQL servers. This works well in decision support applications, where performance is less important than being able to make complex queries.

However, SQL is less appropriate as the sole client/server interface for high-volume on-line transaction processing (OLTP), where a single user transaction, such as accepting an order, may involve many SQL statements to query and update different tables, especially where the client and server are connected by a relatively slow wide area network.

In this situation, the application code for the transaction is usually split. The client code handles the user interface and makes a small number of requests to the server code, which handles database access and is the only part of the code to include SQL statements. The client frequently uses a remote procedure call (RPC) to simplify calling the server. RPC works just like a normal procedure call but operates over a network and provides a simpler way of coding a client/server interaction than if networking facilities were used directly. SQL does not provide any help in making this split, nor does it cause any particular problems. Care should of course be taken to ensure systems are correctly sized to provide adequate performance.

Client/server OLTP systems which require a single transaction to update data on more than one server are covered in section 4.1.3.

4.1.3 Data integration using distributed databases

A distributed database is one in which the physical location of any part of the database, down to individual rows or columns, is transparent to the application. While few products live up to this ideal, some distributed database functionality is available and can be used today.

The primary benefit of using a distributed database is simplified access to data for developers and users. This benefit is obtained at the cost of increased administrative complexity, which together with a lack of distributed database software and software to support the administration of distributed systems has dissuaded most organisations from adopting distributed database technology.

Distributed databases can be used to support the development of applications from scratch. However, a common requirement is to integrate data from legacy and rightsized systems, which poses challenges in terms of transparent access to non-relational data. This integration can be particularly difficult in the case of hierarchical and network model databases.

SQL products can often provide some transparency for queries on distributed databases. However, the technology for choosing the best possible access path through a distributed database, that is distributed query optimisation, is still in its infancy and performance remains a major concern, even if platforms and networks are upgraded.

Transparent update to distributed databases is even more difficult. Although there are inherent trade-offs between correctness and availability in the choice of distributed transaction support technology, few if any products provide this choice.

Whether an application is using a centralised or distributed database, SQL may not be the best client/server interface for high volume OLTP (see section 4.1.2). It may, therefore, be better to use distributed transaction processing (TP) monitors in this case. These monitors coordinate updates to multiple databases from within a single transaction, implemented as a series of RPCs or messages to pieces of server code that include SQL to perform database interaction.

Distributed TP monitors make it possible for each database interaction to be local rather than distributed, by coordinating communications between elements of a distributed TP application, which removes the need for distributed database support for TP applications.

4.1.4 Object-oriented technology and object databases

Object-oriented technology involves eradicating the split between application and data that has been fundamental to computer systems. Objects are small packages of an organisation's data, such as all the data relating to a particular employee, and operations on that data, such as hire, promote and pay. The data in each object can only be accessed and updated by its own operations, leading to a high degree of modularity and to what is hoped will be more maintainable software.

Objects of the same type are grouped into classes, such as 'Employee'. Classes may be structured into an inheritance hierarchy, with each class having one or more parent classes from which they can automatically inherit data and operations. Classes can add their own data and operations to those inherited from parent classes or can redefine the inherited data and operations.

For example, the class 'Salesperson' would inherit from its parent class, 'Employee', and might define an additional data item, 'Commission', as well as re-defining the 'Pay' operation to include the commission in the pay calculation. The application code that processed all employee objects to generate pay cheques would not need to be updated to handle this change of data and processing, because the application code would simply invoke the 'Pay' operation on all employees, whether they were sales people or not.

Inheritance simplifies the reuse of software components, because specialisations of parent classes can be created which inherit data and operations from the parent classes, without changing the latter.

The object-oriented approach to software development is radically different to that adopted in most SQL-based application development. However, an increasing number of organisations are convinced of its benefits and are moving to object-oriented development for certain types of system.

4.1.5 Object database management systems

Object database management systems (ODBMSs) are simply database management systems that allow the direct storage of objects, supporting classes, inheritance hierarchies and complex linkages between objects. ODBMSs are used in applications with very large amounts of highly interconnected data, such as the computer aided design of integrated circuits. However, once ODBMS products are more mature and include the reliability and security features of SQL database products, there will be a strong motivation for object-oriented applications to use ODBMSs. In addition, access to multi-media data, such as sound and video, is somewhat simplified by the more flexible physical structures of object databases.

While many ODBMSs use an SQL interface for ad hoc and other queries, their primary interface is usually object based non-SQL, which avoids writing the equivalent of much of the SQL code that is used in conventional systems for database retrievals and updates.

While there may seem to be a conflict between SQL and object databases, in fact SQL may evolve to include object database technology. The international standards group that produced the SQL-92 standard is now considering the inclusion of objects, classes and inheritance in the next version of the SQL standard. In addition, most vendors of SQL products are planning to produce hybrid object/relational DBMSs which support many of the features of ODBMSs. One such DBMS is already available from a new vendor.

Pure ODBMSs that do not support SQL are unlikely to succeed in mainstream business applications, due to the overwhelming investment in the SQL interface as a means of gaining portability and especially data integration through inter-operability. From a strategic viewpoint, databases that do not support SQL could not easily be integrated with existing relational and non-relational databases and would therefore be less usable by most organisations, except in stand-alone applications.

Given that ODBMSs are currently not mature enough for mainstream business applications and that non-SQL databases would prevent real data integration with legacy systems, it is safe to continue to invest in SQL applications, databases and products, with the rider that object technology should be evaluated for eventual inclusion into an SQL-based technical architecture.

4.2 Standards context of SQL

The world of international IT standards is complex, with many standards of overlapping scope. It is important to understand the positioning of SQL in relation to these other standards, in order to decide when to specify the SQL standard.

This section summarises the standards most closely related to SQL and indicates where they are most applicable. Publicly available specifications are mentioned where no international standard exists, provided that they are not controlled by a single vendor. Such specifications are included because the use of a single publicly available specification in a given area, rather than a number of vendor-controlled standards, greatly simplifies migration to international standards.

In the following subsections, each standard or specification is prefixed where appropriate with the name of the specifying organisation. Its scope and applicability are then summarised. The numbers of international standards are given in the bibliography.

4.2.1 Data management standards

Data management standards are used for managing a coherent, relatively structured set of data, i.e. a structured database, which is usually shared by multiple users using one or more applications:

- International Organization for Standardization (ISO) RDA. This provides access to databases, including SQL databases, using open systems interconnection (OSI) protocols. It is most applicable to low-volume client/server OLTP and to decision support queries on SQL databases, where multi-vendor database products must be used. The SQL-Access Group (SAG) specification for the use of RDA is useful since it enhances inter-operability, has been adopted by most major database vendors and supports TCP/IP protocols (which while more widely available at present, are not as functionally rich as the OSI alternatives). For further details on the RDA standard, please refer to chapter 6

- ISO Information Resource Dictionary System (IRDS). This is a series of standards which will cover the application and user interface to information resource descriptions, typically held in data dictionaries and CASE tool repositories. It includes design support for SQL applications. SQL is used as the applications interface to the dictionary and is also used in specifying parts of the standard itself. For further details on the IRDS standards, please refer to section 6.1.2

- X/Open Index Sequential Access Method (ISAM). This is a CAE specification which specifies the application interface to an ISAM file service. It may be useful as an alternative to SQL for small, stand-alone applications that do not require full database services

Database Language SQL Explained

- American National Standards Institute (ANSI) Z39.50 Information Retrieval Service. This specifies a client/server protocol for access to unstructured textual data as opposed to structured data. It is used as part of the Wide Area Information Servers (WAIS) initiative, which has resulted in several commercial and non-commercial Z39.50 services. Z39.50 is analogous to the combination of SQL and RDA

- Air Transport Association (ATA) Structured Free-text Query Language (SFQL). This specifies an SQL-like query language for access to textual data. It is not related to ANSI Z39.50.

The ISO File Transfer Access Method (FTAM) standard, covered under Communications standards in section 4.2.4, can be used for record-level access to ISAM-like or hierarchical database files.

4.2.2 Data interchange standards

Data interchange standards are used for the interchange of sets of data between applications, where use of a shared database is either impracticable or undesirable, because of incompatible data formats, for example, or for performance or resilience reasons. The interchange standard will define the format and structure of the representation of the data (syntax) and the structure and meaning of the data (semantics).

There are many data interchange standards, most of which are not relevant to SQL applications. Some important types of standard are given below, with examples. Please note that the acronyms have been expanded in the glossary:

- exchange of product design and manufacturing information including graphical data. For example, IGES, PDES/STEP and EDIF

- interchange of data amongst CASE tools and data dictionaries, for example CDIF

- interchange of structured data between organisations, for example EDIFACT

- interchange of textual data between text processing applications, for example ODA/ODIF, SGML and SDIF

- interchange of database information between databases, for example the ISO work on generic database export/import, which covers SQL databases.

4.2.3 Transaction processing standards

Few standards or specifications exist for transaction processing which is still dominated by vendor-controlled interfaces. The key standards are:

- ISO Distributed Transaction Processing (DTP). This is a full international standard which specifies a model, services and protocols used within distributed transaction processing systems. RDA refers to and can work under DTP; DTP uses CCR (see below)

- ISO Commitment, Concurrency and Recovery (CCR). This provides services and protocols that enable the use of distributed transactions. It is used by ISO DTP and FTAM (see section 4.2.4)

- IEEE POSIX 1003.11 Transaction Processing (Application Environment Profile). This effort is not complete but is likely to adopt X/Open DTP specifications (see below) in order to provide standardised application interfaces to TP services

- X/Open Distributed Transaction Processing. This defines a model, application interfaces and other programmable interfaces used within transaction processing systems. It can be used with ISO DTP, but concentrates on the integration of diverse database management systems within a single transaction processing system, whether centralised or distributed.

4.2.4 Communications standards

The ISO Open Systems Interconnection (OSI) standards define a broad range of communications standards covering most requirements. While de facto standards such as TCP/IP and related protocols may be more widely available at present, they are not as functionally rich as the OSI alternatives. Some specific standards, de jure and de facto, are worth mentioning in the context of SQL:

- ISO Remote Procedure Call (RPC). This standardisation work is at an early stage, but will eventually define a standardised mechanism for RPC

- OSF Distributed Computing Environment (DCE). This specifies a number of basic services useful in building client/server applications, including RPC, security, naming and time distribution. It is most relevant to vendors of SQL products but may be used by skilled application developers. RPC is most useful for high volume OLTP using SQL or non-relational databases

- ISO FTAM. This standard includes file access facilities that can be used for record level access to files with an ISAM-style or hierarchical structure. However, current FTAM implementations concentrate on transfer rather than access facilities

- Consultative Committee for International Telephone and Telegraphy (CCITT) X.400 messaging standards. These standards define services for interchange of electronic mail between users or between applications. X.400 can be used for many purposes, including data interchange and application to application communications.

5 International standard for SQL

5.1 SQL standards process

International standards are reviewed approximately every five years or sooner, as necessary. SQL-92 is the second revision of the international standard for SQL and supersedes the previous version SQL-89.

At the working level, international standards are developed by technical experts working voluntarily in the member body countries and meeting together periodically to establish a consensus. The developers of the SQL language are drawn from both database system implementors and from users.

SQL-89 was adopted as a national standard in the UK, the USA, Germany, France, Japan and Canada. It is expected that SQL-92 will similarly be adopted nationally.

5.2 Evolution of the standard

The first international standard for SQL, SQL-87, was produced as a minimal database standard in order to influence the future direction taken by both vendors about to produce SQL implementations and users about to embark on database projects. The approach of standardising a small initial subset, to be expanded later, avoided delays in getting agreement on contents and functionality and proved acceptable to software vendors. Too large an initial standard would have involved vendors in high implementation costs and would therefore have reduced the overall acceptance of the standard. The approach that was taken did, however, result in multiple versions of SQL.

SQL-87 was superseded in 1989 by an upward compatible revision, SQL-89, that incorporated the Integrity Enhancement Feature. The Integrity Enhancement Feature allowed the definition of referential integrity and other simple database constraints. This facility was considered obligatory for any users wishing to use SQL to develop large or complex databases.

Specifically, SQL-89 added the following features to SQL-87:

- referential integrity
- CHECK constraints
- DEFAULT clause excluding the datetime option CURRENT.

The current standard, SQL-92, represents a significant but generally upward compatible enhancement to the facilities provided in SQL-89. These facilities are outlined in section 5.5 and summarised, together with the identified incompatibilities in Annexes B and C.

Work is proceeding on a further revision of the SQL standard, colloquially referred to as SQL3. The contents of SQL3 are not yet fixed but features likely to be included are described in section 9.1.

5.3 Scope of SQL-92

SQL-92 specifies the syntax and semantics of the logical data structures and basic operations for an SQL database. It provides functional capabilities for designing, creating, accessing, maintaining, controlling and protecting the database. It does not cover operation of a database system, for example initiating and terminating a database service, or the mapping of database objects, for example tables, onto operating system entities such as files.

The standard provides a vehicle for portability of database definitions and compilation units between conforming implementations. It also provides a vehicle for interconnecting conforming SQL implementations.

The standard specifies embedded syntax for including SQL statements in a compilation unit that otherwise conforms to the standard of a particular programming language. It defines how an equivalent compilation unit may be derived that conforms to the particular programming language standard. In that equivalent compilation unit, each embedded SQL statement has been replaced by a host language CALL statement that invokes an SQL database procedure. The SQL database procedure contains the SQL statement to be executed.

The standard specifies syntax and semantics for the direct invocation of SQL statements.

The standard does not specify the manner or time of binding between:

- the database management system components
- SQL data definitions
- SQL procedures
- compilation units containing embedded SQL.

SQL-92 does not include application programming languages, end-user query languages, report generators, data dictionary systems, program library systems and distributed communication systems, or tools for database design, data administration and performance optimisation. However, implementations conforming to the standard may exist in environments that support any of these facilities.

5.4 SQL-92 conformance levels

SQL-92 has three conformance levels, each identifying a subset of the complete set of SQL facilities. A higher conformance level identifies a larger subset of facilities than a lower one.

A product claimed to support a particular conformance level must support the facilities identified by the level in the manner described by the SQL-92 standard.

Conformance levels are useful to system designers and application programmers. An application program's usage of SQL facilities may be restricted to those available at a particular conformance level. Such applications should be portable to other SQL implementations providing the same or higher conformance level.

The conformance levels provided in SQL-92 are:

- Entry. This is essentially the same language as that defined in SQL-89, but with some minor corrections and some replacements for language features available in SQL-89 but deprecated in SQL-92 (see Annexes B and C).

  It is provided so that a vendor claiming conformance to SQL-89 may, with minimal effort, claim conformance to SQL-92

- Intermediate. This is a subset of Full SQL, but a significant enhancement of Entry SQL

- Full. This is the complete database language as specified in ISO/IEC 9075:1992 - *Database Language SQL*.

An overview of the major new facilities in SQL-92 is provided in section 5.5 with a detailed description, including levelling, in Annex B.

Claims of conformance must specify the binding styles supported by the implementation and where applicable the programming languages supported.

Three binding styles are specified in the standard:

- Module. Applications written in a standard-conforming host language may explicitly call SQL-procedures which in turn contain the SQL statements to be executed. The SQL-procedures are contained within SQL-modules

- Embedded. The implementation supports SQL statements embedded within standard-conforming programming languages

- Direct invocation. The implementation supports the direct invocation of SQL statements; that is SQL statements invoked other than through a host programming language.

For the module or the embedded binding styles, the programming languages supported by the SQL-92 standard are: Ada, C, COBOL, FORTRAN, MUMPS, Pascal and PL/I. MUMPS is only supported at the Intermediate and Full Conformance Levels.

5.5 Major new facilities in SQL-92

A full list of facilities introduced in the 1992 standard, together with their positioning in SQL-92 conformance levels, is provided in Annex B. However, the following major new categories of facility will be of interest to IT planners and system designers:

- Additional data types. Dates, times and intervals are supported with times maintained in either local or universal coordinated time (UTC) formats.

  Multiple character sets support for stored data includes support for both vendor defined character sets and ISO 10646, the emerging standard for character sets. Character strings can be variable in length

- Connection management. SQL-92 recognises the concept of client and server processors within an SQL environment, allowing a client processor to CONNECT to different SQL-servers. An SQL transaction can extend across a number of servers. When the SQL transaction terminates, the SQL sub-transaction on each of the separate SQL-servers is terminated.

Implementations of the connection management feature are likely to use RDA if it is available, particularly in an open systems environment. RDA is not a necessary prerequisite as proprietary communications could be used if compatible with both the client and the server

- Database integrity features. Various enhancements allow the specification of database integrity rules. Facilities include the specification of inter-table constraints within CHECK clauses, domain definitions, assertion definitions and enhanced referential integrity rules. All database constraints can be named for diagnostic purposes.

  The enhanced database integrity features allow SQL to be used as a sophisticated data modelling language as well as a systems implementation language

- Dynamic SQL. This facility, already available in a number of products, allows SQL program statements to be constructed and executed at application program execution time

- Exception control. SQL-92 introduces a standardised error handling mechanism. The SQL variable SQLSTATE returns standardised error codes. Additional diagnostic information is available in a diagnostic area

- Information Schema. Details of the SQL meta-objects (e.g. tables, columns, constraints) available to an application are provided via a set of SQL views

- Internationalisation. This facility supports applications that span or derive data from wide geographic areas.

  Enhancements to character string data types allow the storage of character data from different character sets. This would for example allow the correct interpretation of names from different languages.

The date-time data types can be defined to interpret dates and times correctly irrespective of time-zone changes.

Names of SQL objects may be defined using alternative character sets

- Relaxation of restrictions. A large number of unnecessary restrictions have been relaxed. Most of these restrictions were included in the SQL-89 standards to accommodate then extant implementations. Examples of restrictions that have been relaxed in SQL-92 are:

    - an insert, update or delete statement that contains a "where" clause is now allowed to reference the subject table of that "where" clause

    - the maximum length of identifiers has been increased from 18 to 128 characters.

6 Related standardisation activities

6.1 SQL-supporting international standards

SQL-92 is a stand alone document. It does not explicitly depend on other standards, although it references the standards for the seven host programming languages supported.

There are a number of international standards in various stages of development which specifically support or reference SQL. An SQL database, however, may exist in an environment that embodies products based on a large number of other standards. In the UK, further information on international, European or national standards is available from the British Standards Institution (BSI).

Guidance on public bodies' obligations to specify standards in procurements is available from CCTA. See also chapter 8.

6.1.1 Remote database access (RDA)

RDA provides standard protocols for establishing remote connections between a database client and a single database server. The RDA standards address the standardisation of distributed processing in a client/server environment.

The RDA specification is a two part standard: Generic RDA for arbitrary database connection and an SQL Specialisation for connecting databases conforming to SQL.

RDA is based on various ISO standards, including the following protocols:

- Association Control Service Element (ACSE)
- Remote Operations Service Element (ROSE)
- Transaction Processing (TP)
- Commitment, Concurrency and Recovery (CCR).

The connection management capabilities in SQL were designed to be consistent with the SQL specialisation of RDA, although SQL support for multiple simultaneous connections requires TP context (two-phase commit) protocols.

Clients and servers conforming to RDA, need to use compatible underlying communication components. (See sections 7.3 and 8.2.)

6.1.2 Information Resource Dictionary System (IRDS)

The Information Resource Dictionary System is a series of standards which will provide a common basis for the development of Information Resource Dictionaries, otherwise known as Data Dictionaries or Systems' Encyclopedia. The standards are current, proposed or under development:

- IRDS Framework. This specifies the overall architecture with respect to its possible data content and its interfaces. The other IRDS standards are partitioned according to the interfaces and data supported. The IRDS Framework is *ISO/IEC 10027:1990* which is being revised

- IRDS Services Interface. The IRDS Services Interface Standard defines the IRDS facilities required to provide the following:

    - extensibility of the IRDS data content

    - data integrity at all levels

    - auditing at each stage in the systems' life cycle

    - control of access to the IRDS

  IRDS Services may be used by CASE tool builders to facilitate the integration of tools. The Services Interface standard is *ISO/IEC 10728:1993*

- various standards that extend the data content of the IRDS to support other prescribed ISO standards. For example:

    - SQL

    - programming languages such as COBOL, Pascal and Ada

    - other related standards such as Directory Services

- IRDS Import/Export Interface. This allows IRDS definitions to be moved from one IRDS environment to another.

The item of particular relevance to SQL is the standard which extends the data content to support SQL and which provides design support for SQL applications. This standard is under development but its release is not imminent.

As well as potentially being supported by IRDS, SQL is used in the definition of IRDS standards. For example, SQL is used as the data modelling language within the IRDS Services Interface Standard to describe the content of IRDS objects and the relationships that exist between them. It is likely, but not mandatory, that early IRDS implementations, when and if they are developed, will be based on SQL.

6.1.3 Export/import

Work is in progress for a generic database export/import standard for SQL databases, together with a specialisation of that standard. Export/Import for SQL will allow the transfer of SQL data and/or schema objects. The Export/Import standard, whose SQL specialisation may become part of the SQL3 standard, is expected to specify a syntax for initiating or receiving a transfer, together with a specification of the information interchange format. This work is in a very early stage of its development

6.2 Consortia standardisation bodies

There are a number of vendor consortia producing SQL specifications. These vendor consortia provide input to, and take notice of the international standard. However, their specifications, while generally compatible with the international standard, are not necessarily identical to it. Generally vendor consortia specifications reflect what their constituent members wish to implement.

6.2.1 SQL-Access Group

The SQL-Access Group (SAG), set up in 1989, is a vendor consortium which includes virtually all the major and many minor database implementors.

Originally SAG was formed to demonstrate inter-operability of SQL systems using RDA. In particular, it implemented a prototype RDA using particular PICS proforma to connect SQL systems from a number of vendors. This work was subsequently published by X/Open as a snapshot technical specification. This specification was not complete, and did not fully represent the ISO RDA or SQL standards. However, it did include implementation details beyond those found in the ISO RDA standard. It is expected to be revised to be compatible with the approved ISO standard.

SAG's work in producing a prototype implementation of RDA required vendors to have available subsets of facilities defined in SQL-92, which had not been available within the XPG3 SQL specification.

SAG has become a more general forum for SQL language development, working on other aspects of the SQL language, in particular, a Call Level Interface (CLI) specification, an important facility to vendors of 'shrink wrapped' software. It will be sponsored by ANSI as a candidate for SQL3 but is likely to be fast-tracked as an addendum to SQL-92 and be published in 1995. The CLI specification will be compatible with SQL-92.

6.2.2 X/Open

X/Open is an international public limited company promoting vendor and user interests in the area of open systems. It was originally set up as a forum of European vendors by Bull, ICL, Siemens, Olivetti and Nixdorf in the mid 1980's, but now all the major database vendors are represented. Entry criteria based on turnover exclude a number of the smaller software suppliers; CCTA is a member of the User Council of X/Open. X/Open's database interests are wider than just SQL.

X/Open periodically publishes Common Application Environment (CAE) specifications of SQL and other system environment components; the content of these CAE specifications is agreed by participating vendors and represents language features implemented by the majority of those vendors.

X/Open's CAE Specification for SQL is based on Entry SQL-92, but differs in that it makes support of the Integrity Enhancement Feature optional and does not directly implement the CREATE SCHEMA statement. X/Open states its intention to make these items mandatory in future. The embedded binding style is only provided for C and COBOL. In addition, some features are supported from Intermediate and Full SQL-92 such as connection management, dynamic SQL, temporary tables and the information schema. These facilities are compatible subsets of the corresponding facilities in SQL-92. The CAE Specification also includes features which are not included in SQL-92 at any conformance level.

Currently the X/Open specification for SQL does not correspond exactly to any particular conformance level in SQL-92, but it is hoped that eventually the X/Open SQL specification will be completely compatible with Full SQL-92.

In the meantime, compatibility could be a problem in an environment using equipment conforming to both the international standard and the X/Open CAE Specification.

Following an agreement between X/Open and SAG, X/Open now acts as a publishing forum for SAG specifications and used the SAG specification for SQL within the CAE specification for SQL. Currently SAG initiated developments form the majority of SQL and RDA work undertaken by X/Open.

6.2.3 Structured Full-text Query Language

Structured Full-text Query language (SFQL) is the draft specification of a language for retrieving textual information in a device-independent manner from CD-ROM and other such devices. SFQL was devised within the airline industry under the auspices of the Air Transport Association (ATA) to provide a standard access method to maintenance manuals and other information on aircraft engines.

The details are found in document ATA89 - 9C. SFQL 2, version 2, revision 2, July 1991: *CD-ROM Interchangeability Standard - Structured Free Text Query Language (SFQL)*.

Original versions of SFQL were not like SQL. Version 2, revision 2 more closely resembles the retrieval capabilities of the SQL language, but with many major SQL features missing. SFQL does, however, incorporate facilities for the retrieval and handling of large volumes of text.

Further information is available from the Air Transport Association, Washington DC, USA.

7 Conformance and timescales

7.1 Conformance testing and vendor claims

Vendors claiming conformance to a national or international standard should generally be claiming conformance to the current version of that standard though, in a transition period, vendors may qualify the conformance to indicate that their products conform to a superseded version of the standard.

Standards usually require additional information to be specified in their *Conformance clause*, to qualify any claim to conformance. Claims of conformance are important and the information provided by the vendor should be checked against that required by the referenced standard. Vendors should be required to make available any applicable validation reports on request.

Claims of conformance can be substantiated only if the product has passed an approved conformance test suite. Conformance testing is an important issue and it is hoped that in the future test suites will be developed in parallel with standards development.

Testing services for national and international standards are usually operated by bodies such as the National Institute of Standards and Technology (NIST) in the USA or the National Computing Centre (NCC) in the UK. Vendor consortia, such as X/Open, may operate their own conformance testing service to authenticate claims of conformance to their own specifications.

Conformance tests validate products for their correct interpretation of the syntax and semantics specified by the relevant standard. Conformance testing does not mean, however, that products will interwork. **SQL conformance test suites do not test performance; nor do they necessarily test capacity.** A product's conformance to a standard therefore cannot be assumed to imply that the product will perform well in an operational environment.

7.2 SQL-92 conformance claims and testing

Vendors' claims of conformance to SQL-92 should specify the conformance level, the host programming languages and, for each host programming language, the style of binding supported by their products (see section 5.4).

However, during the transition period, some vendors may claim conformance to the superseded standard, SQL-89, with or without the Integrity Enhancement Feature, rather than to SQL-92, in which case they should specify whether their products conform to level 1 or level 2.

Currently, the only recognised conformance testing service for SQL is operated by NIST in the USA though, both X/Open and the NCC may offer some form of service in the future. While the NIST conformance test suite was originally constructed to validate SQL products against ANSI standards, passing the ANSI conformance test suite implies conformance to the corresponding identical ISO standard.

Products passing the NIST conformance test suite will appear in NIST's Validated Product List (VPL), a document that is updated every three months. This is available on subscription from National Technical Information Service (NTIS) in the USA. CCTA will hold an up to date reference copy. Detailed test results for each product are contained in Validation Summary Reports (VSR) which are available from NIST.

As of January 1993, the NIST test suite only checked conformance of SQL implementations to SQL-89. However, it is expected that a test suite for Entry SQL-92 will become available later in 1993. Following that it will be enhanced to test for packages of functionality, such as date and time, dynamic SQL, RDA/SQL client and RDA/SQL server. This approach to testing is likely to be consistent with the way major vendors release new SQL facilities.

7.3 RDA conformance testing

Currently, there are no conformance tests available for RDA; the ISO RDA standard was approved in 1992. When users raise conformance as an important issue, conformance tests are likely to be developed to test RDA in a particular context, for example, RDA/SQL client, RDA/SQL server. Conformance testing will take the form of monitoring the messages passing between a client and a server to see that they conform to the RDA specification. It is likely that NIST will provide an SQL-RDA conformance testing service by 1995.

7.4 Timescales for SQL-92

Vendors of new DBMS products will not be constrained by previous architectures and will not have to divert development resources to maintain compatibility with existing products. These vendors will have an advantage over those with established products in being able to move more quickly to implement new SQL facilities. However, SQL-92 is significantly larger than SQL-89 and so even for these vendors, implementation timescales will be protracted.

Implementations of Full SQL-92 are unlikely to appear from major database vendors until the second half of the decade. SQL3 is unlikely to be published as a full standard before 1997 although it is most likely that some SQL3 features will be published as addenda to SQL-92.

Nevertheless, all major database software vendors are associated with the SQL standards development process, either directly through their national standards bodies or through vendor consortia such as X/Open. Therefore, the content of the SQL-92 standard did not come as a surprise and a number of vendors were well on the way to implementing some of the new features.

All vendors will implement and release new SQL features incrementally, dependent on user demand.

7.5 Timescales for RDA

It is likely that implementations of RDA, probably of limited scope or application, will be available soon. Many of the major database vendors have been involved, either directly or indirectly, in developing the standard and a number of vendors participating in SAG have demonstrated inter-operability with prototype SQL/RDA systems.

8 SQL, RDA and procurements

The European Council IT Standards Decision 87/95/EEC requires member states to ensure that references are made to European standards or prestandards, or international standards, in public procurement orders exceeding a value of 100,000 ECU relating to information technology.

This Decision applies to standards used as the basis for the exchange of information and data for systems inter-operability. The Decision is not restricted to central government. Other public sector bodies covered by the Decision include local government, education, police and fire authorities, new town corporations and EEC funded bodies. Failure to comply with this Decision could lead to challenge and halted procurements.

In any event the use of international, European, or national standards, (or if none of these exists, of publicly available specifications) facilitates systems' inter-operability and helps preserve organisations' investment in software and systems. Unless there are overwhelming reasons to the contrary, SQL should be specified as a component of any government organisation's policies for open systems and data management.

8.1 Procurements involving SQL

Government organisations requiring SQL databases should thus generally have a policy of seeking standards-conforming products, but particularly if any of the following are true:

- the procurement is subject to the Public Supply Contract Regulations 1991 relating to the use of standards in public procurements

- portability is a requirement

- client/server inter-operability, in particular involving RDA, is a requirement.

From 1 January 1994, government organisations procuring SQL-based databases or related products should require, as a minimum, that products conform to Entry SQL-92 (ISO 9075:1992).

In circumstances where IS planners and purchasers decide that the XPG4 CAE Specification for SQL provides a solution or migration path that better meets the immediate needs of an individual project, compliance with the CAE Specification should be specified as highly desirable. In order to comply with the EC public procurement legislation this requirement should not be made mandatory, unless a valid overriding technical or economic case for doing so can be established.

Further, government organisations should be aware that, because the CAE specification places additional requirements on the supplier, the differences between SQL-92 and the CAE Specification could cause compatibility problems.

Until 31 December 1993, government organisations should continue to require conformance to SQL-89.

Government organisations should require vendors to state their policy towards SQL conformance in general and to indicate to which SQL conformance levels their products have been successfully tested. Some vendors may continue to claim conformance to SQL-89 during a transition period, which could last until the end of 1994.

Products are unlikely to offer proven conformance to higher than Entry SQL-92 in the near future. Where facilities are required from the Intermediate or Full conformance levels then government organisations should specify the precise subset of facilities required from these higher conformance levels. It may be necessary to accept a subset of the facilities defined in SQL-92.

Chapter 8
SQL, RDA and procurements

8.1.1 Application portability

IS planners and purchasers need to be aware that conforming to an SQL standard aids application portability but does not guarantee it.

Implementation-defined limits may restrict application portability. Application portability may also be compromised if applications incorporate vendor-specific extensions to SQL or if they depend on components other than standard programming languages.

Where application portability is a significant issue, then IS purchasers are recommended to procure products containing the *flagger facility*.

The flagger facility, required for conformance at the Intermediate and Full levels in SQL-92, flags any application statement that is using facilities provided by the product that are beyond or otherwise inconsistent with the standard at SQL compilation time. Compiling an application using a flagger facility will identify application SQL statements that may restrict the application's portability. Many products, in particular those sold into the US Government market, have a flagger that operates at Entry level as well as at higher conformance levels.

8.1.2 Implementation defined limits

There are a number of implementation characteristics that are classified as *implementation defined*. Within the SQL standard it is not possible to standardise such characteristics, for example the maximum length of a row in a table or the maximum precision of an integer.

IS purchasers therefore need to confirm by reference to supplier's documentation that tendered products do not contain implementation-defined restrictions or limits incompatible with their requirements.

A list of implementation-defined characteristics applicable to an SQL processor are defined in an annex in the SQL-92 standard.

8.1.3	Additional requirements	Additional requirements such as end-user query facilities, application generators, dictionary facilities and report writers are outside the scope of the SQL standard and will need to be specified separately.
8.1.4	Performance testing	**As conformance validation does not test performance, separate performance tests, possibly devised as part of the procurement, or other contractual guarantees are necessary to ensure that products perform adequately in a specified environment.**
8.2	Procurements involving RDA	IS purchasers requiring inter-operability in a client/server environment involving servers and/or clients from different vendors should prefer suppliers pledged to implement RDA-conforming products. Such products will only interwork if their underlying communication components are compatible.
		Products should successfully pass the official RDA conformance tests when these are available. In the absence of official tests, independent tests provided by vendor consortia may be acceptable.
		IS purchasers should require vendors, who claim RDA conformance for their products, to demonstrate inter-operability through a Protocol Implementation Conformance Statement (PICS) proforma approach. Although it is not a guarantee of inter-operability, two implementations of RDA will only work together if their corresponding PICS proformas are compatible.

9 Future developments of SQL

SQL3, the colloquial name for the development work on the replacement for the SQL-92 standard, has been under way for some time and a number of facilities that were proposed initially as candidates for the SQL-92 standard have been deferred to SQL3.

While the content of SQL3 is not fixed, it is likely that SQL3 will be much more object-orientated than SQL-92. Object-orientation is an approach that may in the future make the designing and implementation of complex systems easier.

The enhanced access control and database integrity features will be important in guaranteeing the integrity of the very complex databases that are likely to become the norm in the future.

9.1 SQL3 facilities

The following facilities are under review for inclusion in SQL3:

- user-defined abstract data types. These are abstract data types whose characteristics are user-defined and may be specified within SQL. Functions may be defined to implement the behaviour of instances of the data type. Columns of an abstract data type may have an encapsulation level specified for them

- objects. An *object* in SQL3 is a user-defined abstract data type for which every instance of the data type has an associated object identifier. Objects are subject to special *constructor* and *destructor* operations that create new instances of the object and destroy occurrences of the object

- subtypes and inheritance. Inheritance is an abstraction mechanism that adds to the power of data abstraction by allowing classes of objects to be related hierarchically. Operations on supertypes automatically relate to their subtypes

- generalised trigger mechanism. These are triggers which allow database operations to be automatically initiated by other database operations. This type of facility is useful for maintaining database integrity and to enhance encapsulation

- roles and security. Within SQL-92, all users are considered as separate entities for privilege definition purposes. Managing such a system becomes difficult when handling large user communities. In SQL3, *Roles* may be defined that allow users to be grouped by their role or function and privileges allocated in terms of those roles

- save points and sub-transactions. SQL-92 contains provision for two levels of rollback within a transaction:

    - statement level rollback. This is invoked automatically if a statement terminates in error

    - transaction level rollback. This is invoked if an application or user does not issue a COMMIT at the end of a transaction

    Within SQL3, an application can define intra-transaction *save points* and thereby pre-commit or rollback a part of a transaction. This capability is particularly useful in interactive "what if" sessions

- control structures. In SQL-92, SQL procedures contain only a single SQL statement. All temporary state and flow control is provided by the host programming language. SQL3, however, allows SQL procedures to contain multiple SQL statements, together with control flow and exception handling capabilities

- enumerated data types. The enumerated data type provides facilities similar to those provided in languages such as Pascal

- multiple null states. SQL data types, unless specifically defined otherwise, may be null. The null state is typically used to indicate that a value is either missing, perhaps not known or not relevant. However, statistical applications frequently need to distinguish between such states and multiple null states provide that capability

- generalised assertion mechanism. Assertions allow the specification of integrity predicates on database states and changes of state

- external procedures. These allow an application to invoke routines defined outside the database environment

- asynchronous DDL and DML. Asynchronous operation allows an application to initiate SQL statements that are executed concurrently

- primary key inheritance and join updatability. Primary keys may be inherited by derived tables, thereby adding to the semantic content of the data and allowing the relaxation of rules on join updatability

- temporary views. These are views whose definition lasts only for the duration of an SQL session

- processing of tree structured data. Recursive table derivation necessary to process tree structured data used in applications such as Bill of Materials or Management hierarchies.

The abstract data type provisions open up the possibility that application specific *packages* of abstract data types and their associated processing procedures may be developed. Candidates for such packages are application areas with well defined data handling requirements such as general text management and geographical information systems.

9.2 Timescales for SQL3

The revision of the SQL standard, SQL3, is unlikely to appear as a full ISO standard before 1997, though it is probable that packages addressing specific functional areas will be released earlier. These releases are likely to take the form of addenda to SQL-92.

Vendors are likely to introduce SQL3 compliant facilities into their products as *language extensions* before SQL3 becomes a standard. Some features will appear in industry consortia standards such as those from X/Open. These features are likely to be available in a range of products. Other features will be introduced by individual vendors to serve their own market needs.

Annex A: SQL standards documents

This annex identifies the various national and international SQL standards documents that are frequently referred to either in the press or by vendors. It also notes where these documents correspond.

A.1 International standard

The current international SQL standard (SQL-92) (English text) is:

ISO/IEC 9075:1992 (E), *Database Language SQL*

Earlier, now superseded international standards were:

ISO/IEC 9075:1989 (E), *Database Language SQL*

ISO/IEC 9075:1987 (E), *Database Language SQL*

A.2 National standards

As mentioned in section 5.1, SQL standards appear under a number of national variants. The ANSI standards are the ones most commonly encountered in the press and in software vendor literature:

ANSI X3-135: 1992, *Database Language SQL*. This is identical in normative text to ISO/IEC 9075:1992.

ANSI X3-135: 1989, *Database Language SQL*. This was almost identical in normative text to ISO/IEC 9075:1989. The only significant difference was that the embedded language bindings for COBOL, FORTRAN, Pascal and PL/I were made normative in the ANSI standard. They had been annexes (and therefore non-normative in the formal ISO sense) in the ISO standard

ANSI X3-135: 1986, *Database Language SQL*. This was identical in normative text to ISO/IEC 9075:1987.

The current and superseded variants of the standard have also been defined as British standards. The text is identical to the corresponding international standard, except for a national foreword. The corresponding current BS standard is:

BS 6964:1992

The superseded standards are:

BS 6964:1989, BS 6964:1987.

A.3   **Vendor specifications**   SQL, as defined in X/Open's Portability Guide XPG3 is defined from ANSI X3-135:1986 but includes some minor restrictions. The incompatibilities with the corresponding ISO and ANSI standards are documented in an annex.

X/Open's XPG4 CAE Specification for SQL is based on Entry SQL-92. Details of how they differ are given in section 6.2.2.

A.4   **FIPS PUBS**   Within the US, Federal departments and agencies are generally required to procure products conforming to Federal Information Processing Standards Publications (FIPS PUBS). FIPS PUBS are issued by NIST and available from NTIS. FIPS PUB 127-1 corresponded generally to US standard ANSI X3.135:1989, the main exceptions being:

- PL/I language bindings are not included. PL/I is not a FIPS programming language
- FIPS 127-1 does not recognise conformance solely by direct invocation
- FIPS 127-1 requires an SQL Flagger facility
- The Integrity Enhancement feature is optional.

FIPS 127-2, effective from July 1993, is based upon SQL-92 rather than SQL-89. Conformance to FIPS 127-2 at Entry level requires conformance to the requirements of FIPS 127-1 together with:

- the Integrity Enhancement feature

- SQLSTATE status codes which are standardised error and warning codes returned via the SQL variable SQLSTATE

- delimited identifier, which is the ability to delimit identifiers explicitly, so allowing the use of reserved words or words containing special symbols as identifiers

- renaming columns in a select list which allows columns named in a select list to be referenced by name in a sort specification. SQL-89 required that sort columns could only be referenced by their ordinal position in the select list. Numeric column references in a sort specification is a deprecated feature in SQL-92

- comma delimited parameter lists - SQL-89 separated parameters in a <declaration list> by spaces. Separation by spaces is a deprecated feature in SQL-92

- SQL errata - various corrections and amendments to SQL-89.

Annex B: SQL-92 facilities

This annex lists the new facilities included in each of the three SQL-92 conformance levels. These facilities are derived from the list of proposals accepted during the standard's development. It is necessary to consult the standard for a full understanding of the implications of various changes to SQL-89 facilities.

B.1 Entry SQL-92

SQL-89   Includes the whole of ISO/IEC 9075:1989, except where modified by the areas noted below:

Module language   Conformance through module language bindings requires support for at least one of the six optional languages: Ada, C, COBOL, FORTRAN, Pascal, PL/I.

Embedded language   Conformance through embedded language bindings requires support for at least one of the six optional languages: Ada, C, COBOL, FORTRAN, Pascal, PL/I.

Replacements for deprecated features   The term *deprecated* is used in SQL-92 to mean that the feature so labelled may not be supported in some future revision of the SQL standard but is a fully supported and required feature of SQL-92:

SQLSTATE - SQLSTATE replaces SQLCODE, which is now a deprecated feature, to provide standardised error handling

Renaming columns in a select list - allows deprecation of numeric column references

Comma separated parameter lists - allows deprecation of space separated parameters.

	Corrections	**Approximate numeric clarification** - rules concerning overflow have been clarified
		Implicit ROLLBACK on program termination - if a program terminates abnormally, rollback is assured
		Exception in numeric expressions - some restrictions have been relaxed
		Name space clarification - clarification on the availability of names is provided.
	Incompatibilities with SQL-89	**Preceding colons for parameter names** - this is a usability aid allowing programs to be read more easily
		Interpretation of nested WITH CHECK - incompatible correction to an earlier error.
	Transition aids	Transition aids are facilities to help application programmers migrate applications from products conforming to an earlier version of the standard to products conforming to the current version.
		Delimited identifiers - this facility removes the problem of newly introduced key words clashing with identifiers in existing programs.
B.2	Intermediate SQL-92	All of Entry SQL-92 together with:
	Exception control	**Diagnostic area support** - additional information will be provided following an exception
		CLASS/SUBCLASS_ORIGIN in diagnostic area - naming authority that returned exception code
		Constraint names - constraints will now be named and names will be returned in the diagnostic area
		Exception handling in character expressions - exception handling in character expressions has been clarified.

Orthogonality and removal of restrictions	**Lower case identifiers and key words** - identifiers and key words can now be upper or lower case. Upper and lower case Latin letters inside non-delimited identifiers are considered identical
	128 character identifiers - the maximum length of identifiers has been increased from 18 to 128 characters
	Relaxed union compatibility - the very strict restrictions in SQL-89, that for example character strings needed to be of the same length, have been dropped
	Separation of UNIQUE and NOT NULL - the constraint UNIQUE no longer implies NOT NULL
	Relaxation of rules for query expressions - query expressions are permitted in subqueries, views and INSERT statements
	Subquery allowed in value expressions - scalar subqueries are allowed in value expressions
	Value expression in LIKE - LIKE predicates may now contain value expressions
	Relax cursor update rule - there has been a minor relaxation of restrictions; a "where" clause can include a subquery providing the subquery does not reference the table underlying the view
	COUNT ALL - the ALL option is now allowed on the COUNT function.

Access control	**Privilege definition clarification** - the meaning of multiple privilege definitions and the REVOKING of the "WITH GRANT OPTION" have been clarified
	Separation of schema name and authorization identifier - are two separately specifiable concepts
	SET USER AUTHORIZATION statement - sets the current user authorization identifier
	USAGE privilege for domains - controls who can use a domain.
Other miscellaneous features	**Ordering of cursor rows** - the reproduction of the ordering of rows of a cursor is guaranteed
	Assignment of an approximate numeric to exact numeric - this is now allowed
	DISTINCT function restriction removed - value specification has been allowed in the DISTINCT set function
	SYSTEM USER & SESSION USER - access to operating system and session user names is allowed.
Dynamic SQL	**Dynamic SQL statements** - preparation, (i.e. compiling at application program execution time), and execution of DDL/DML statements and a functional interface to descriptor areas is provided.
Schema manipulation	**Schema manipulation language** - a schema manipulation language is now provided
	DROP SCHEMA statement - a facility to allow a schema to be dropped
	CASCADE option for DROP commands - DROP commands may optionally be cascaded, for example, DROPping a table will drop associated views.

Schema information table	**Schema information tables** - views on schema information tables are available to allow identification of the tables and columns available to an authorization identifier and to enable determination of the effect of cascaded schema manipulation operations.
Data types	**Datetime data type** - datetime data types DATE, TIME and TIMESTAMP have been introduced. Datetime data is stored as either local or UTC time
	Interval data type - an interval data type is definable
	National character set support - provides support for one implementation-defined character repertoire in addition to the set of characters supporting and used in the SQL language. Identifiers are definable using national characters
	CHARACTER VARYING data type - variable length character strings are allowed with maximum length specification
	Derived C type CHARACTER VARYING - the handling of variable length strings in C has been clarified
	INTEGER and SMALLINT as COBOL parameters.
Scalar operators and functions	**CASE expressions** - expressions of the form CASE... WHEN are permitted
	COALESCE - allows the selection of the first non-null value from a set of values
	NULLIF - a function on a parameter producing the result NULL if the parameter has a specific value
	String functions - substring and concatenate functions are provided
	LENGTH functions - returns the length of a character or bit string
	CAST operator - allows conversion (CASTing) either to comparable data types or to/from a character string.

Relational objects	**Domains** - definition of domains; checking domain compatibility in expressions
	Row value expressions - expressions whose result is a row rather than a value.
Relational operations	**Join operators** - explicit join, outer join (left, right and full) and natural join
	Set operators - intersection, difference operator, outer union and inner set operator CORRESPONDING.
Integrity control	**Referential actions - cascade delete** - deleting a row cascades to any referencing rows which are themselves deleted and the referencing value set to NULL or to a default value.
Usability options	**Multiple module support** - applications can now comprise more than one module
	SCROLL cursors - cursors where an application has control over the next row fetched.
Convenience items	**PRIMARY KEY implies NOT NULL** - following the separation of UNIQUE and NOT NULL, PRIMARY KEY implies NOT NULL
	UNIQUE predicate - tests if the rows of a table are distinct
	Sort by derived column - sorting by a derived column which is a value expression in a cursor is allowed.
Performance options	**Read only transactions** - a declaration that a transaction will not update the database
	Transaction isolation levels - allows the specification of reduced consistency requirements with respect to concurrent database updates
	Read only/update cursors - cursors can now be defined as READ ONLY.

	Other miscellaneous features	**SET LOCAL TIME ZONE statement** - allows the specification of the local time zone applicable to an application
		MUMPS language support - support for the MUMPS language (MUMPS is levelled into Intermediate SQL-92 rather than Entry SQL-92 because MUMPS requires variable length character strings which are not available in Entry SQL-92).
B.3	Full SQL-92	All of Intermediate SQL-92 together with:
	Dynamic SQL	**Enhanced support for dynamic SQL** - variable descriptor names and occurrences; variable identifiers and cursor names; <deallocate prepare statement>; <dynamic single row select statement>; <preparable positioned dynamic delete> and <preparable positioned dynamic update> statements are now provided
		SET CATALOG and SCHEMA statements - set the default catalogue name and schema name substitution values for unqualified schema names in preparable statements
		SET NAMES statement - sets the default character set name substitution value for identifiers and character string literals in preparable statements.
	Schema manipulation	**DROP ASSERTION** - drop an assertion; assertions occur in Full SQL-92 only
		ALTER DOMAIN statement - alter the descriptor of a domain.
	Schema information tables	Schema information tables associated with assertions and constraints.

Orthogonality and removal of restrictions	**Lift restriction on grouped views** - removal of the implementation restrictions on where grouped views are allowed to appear
	Multiple DISTINCT in SELECT - allows DISTINCT to appear more than once in a query expression, select statement, or subquery
	Derived tables in FROM - table expressions in the FROM part of a table expression are allowed
	Self referencing updates, inserts and deletes - allow an update, insert or delete statement to have a "where" clause that references the subject table
	Trailing underscore in identifiers - allows identifiers of the form X_.
	Value expression restrictions lifted - value expressions in IN predicates and in DISTINCT set functions are allowed.
Data types and character sets	**Multiple character set support** - USAGE privileges for character sets, collating sequences and translations; pre-defined character translations; form-of-use conversions; pre-defined collating sequences; Translation collation; <introducer> escape mechanism
	BIT data type, BIT strings and associated functions - data, literals and functions of type BIT are allowed.
Predicates	**MATCH predicate** - a new predicate mirroring the implied predicate used in referential constraints
	Truth value search conditions - Boolean literals TRUE, FALSE and UNKNOWN.
Connection management statement	**Clients and Servers** - CONNECT/DISCONNECT/SET CONNECTION statements
	Multiple server transactions - transactions spanning multiple servers; two-phase commit.

Annex B
SQL-92 facilities

Scalar operators and functions	**POSITION function** - position of a string in another
	UPPER and LOWER functions - character string case translation functions.
Relational objects	**Row expressions** - generalised row expressions
	Table value expressions - expressions whose result is a table rather than a value
	Simplified assertions - constraints not associated with a particular table.
Relational operations	**CROSS JOIN, Inner Set Corresponding and Outer Union** - additional set operators and type operators for processing tables.
Integrity control	**MATCH option on referential integrity** - provides control over whether matching rows in referential constraints is determined by full keys or partial keys
	Referential actions - cascade update - changing a referenced value cascades on update operations. Any referencing columns are either updated to the same value, set to NULL or set to a default value
	Cascaded/local CHECK option - clarifies the way in which the WITH CHECK OPTION operates for views
	Deferred constraint checking - defers constraint checking to a time specified by the user and allows the population of cyclic constraints
	Assertions - table independent constraints are allowed
	Subquery in CHECK clause - allows a subquery to appear in a CHECK clause.
Access control	**Column specific INSERT privileges** - assignment of insert privileges at the column level are now allowed
	REFERENCES privilege for CHECK clause - a new privilege allowing referencing, but not select access to data.

Usability options	**Insensitive cursors** - provides the ability to define a cursor that is unaffected by database operations other than those actioned through that cursor
	TABLE key word - shorthand for SELECT * FROM
	Temporary tables - tables whose content is defined for a session only
	Global temporary tables - temporary tables which are shared between modules.
Naming schema objects	**Schema name qualification** - schema names which are qualifiable by a catalogue name.

Annex C: Migrating applications from SQL-89 to SQL-92

C.1 Compatibility of Entry SQL-92 with SQL-89

In general SQL-92 is upward compatible with SQL-89, with the exception of the corrections and interpretations identified in Annex B: Entry SQL-92. There are however other minor incompatibilities which are listed in an annex of SQL-92. These are:

- SQL-89 allowed an INSERT statement to insert the value NULL into any column in a table. SQL-92 requires that the column allows the storage of null values

- SQL-89 stated that after the last call to the DBMS by a programming agent, the choice as to whether to do a commit or rollback was implementor defined. In SQL-92 this has been clarified to say that if an error occurs, then a rollback is performed

- In SQL-89, indicator variables were set to reflect the length of a non-null character string that was the source for a parameter only if truncation had occurred. In SQL-92 they always indicate the length of a non-null string

- In SQL-89, the definition of the comment introducer "--" was ambiguous in that "---" could be taken to mean minus followed comment. In SQL-92, the string "---" is now defined as comment introducing a comment which happened to be a "-" character

- SQL-92 reserves approximately one hundred new keywords. These are specified in Annex D.

C.2 Migration

Applications written for an SQL-89 conforming environment will generally continue to produce identical results in an SQL-92 environment available from the same database vendor.

SQL-89 applications that generate error conditions are unlikely to be simply migratable to a database environment (conforming to either SQL-89 or SQL-92) from another vendor as error reporting, through SQLCODE, was not standardised in SQL-89.

SQL-89 applications that use SQL-92 keywords as identifiers will require changing. Those identifiers corresponding to keywords may either be rewritten as delimited identifiers or changed.

Otherwise, the language incompatibilities between SQL-89 and SQL-92 are very minor and are unlikely to affect most programs.

Annex D: New reserved keywords

The SQL-92 standard reserves approximately one hundred new keywords. This is in addition to those already reserved by SQL-89.

Application programmers should avoid using reserved keywords as identifiers. This point applies to the development of SQL-89 as well as SQL-92 conforming applications since any new reserved keywords used as identifiers in SQL-89 conforming applications may need modifying when the application is migrated to an SQL-92 environment.

The following are new reserved keywords:

ABSOLUTE	CORRESPONDING
ACTION	CROSS
ADD	CURRENT_DATE
ALLOCATE	CURRENT_TIME
ALTER	CURRENT_TIMESTAMP
ARE	
ASSERTION	CURRENT_USER
AT	DATE
BIT	DAY
BIT_LENGTH	DEALLOCATE
BOTH	DEFERRABLE
CASCADE	DEFERRED
CASCADED	DESCRIBE
CASE	DESCRIPTOR
CAST	DIAGNOSTICS
CATALOG	DISCONNECT
CHAR_LENGTH	DOMAIN
CHARACTER_LEN	DROP
COALESCE	ELSE
COLLATE	EXCEPT
COLLATION	EXCEPTION
COLUMN	EXECUTE
CONNECT	EXTERNAL
CONNECTION	EXTRACT
CONSTRAINT	FALSE
CONSTRAINTS	FIRST
CONVERT	FULL

GET	SCROLL
GLOBAL	SECOND
HOUR	SESSION
IDENTITY	SESSION_USER
IMMEDIATE	SIZE
INNER	SQLSTATESUBSTRING
INPUT	SYSTEM_USER
INSENSITIVE	TEMPORARY
INTERSECT	THEN
INTERVAL	TIME
ISOLATION	TIMESTAMP
JOIN	TIMEZONE_HOUR
LAST	TIMEZONE_MINUTE
LEADING	TRAILING
LEFT	TRANSACTION
LEVEL	TRANSLATE
LOCAL	TRANSLATION
LOWER	TRIM
MATCH	TRUE
MINUTE	UNKNOWN
MONTH	UPPER
NAMES	USAGE
NATIONAL	USING
NATURAL	VALUE
NCHAR	VARCHAR
NEXT	VARYING
NO	WHEN
NULLIF	WRITE
OCTET_LENGTH	YEAR
ONLY	ZONE
OUTER	
OUTPUT	
OVERLAPS	
PAD	
PARTIAL	
POSITION	
PREPARE	
PRESERVE	
PRIOR	
READ	
RELATIVE	
RESTRICT	
REVOKE	
RIGHT	
ROWS	

Bibliography

Information Systems Guides	The Information Systems Guides, published by CCTA are available from John Wiley & Sons Ltd, Baffins Lane, Chichester PO19 1UD. Tel: 0243 779777.
	The following set of IS Guides is referenced in this volume:
	IS Guides B Set: Systems Development Set
Policy Statement	IS Standards: Policy for UK Public Sector Organisations
	Copies can be obtained from the CCTA Library. Tel: 071 217 3331.
International Organization for Standardization	The following ISO standards are referenced in this volume:

ISO/IEC 8571	File Transfer, Access and Management
ISO/IEC 8613	ODA/ODIF
ISO/IEC 8650	Association Control Service Element protocol
ISO/IEC 9069: 1988	SGML Document Interchange Format (SDIF)
ISO/IEC 9072	Remote Operations Service Element protocol
ISO/IEC 9075: 1992	Database Language SQL
ISO/IEC 9075: 1989	SQL-1 with addendum
ISO/IEC 9579 - 1	Remote Database Access - Part 1, Generic model, service and protocol

ISO/IEC 9579 - 2	Remote Database Access - Part 2, SQL specialisation
ISO/IEC 9735:1990	Electronic data interchange for administration, commerce and transport (EDIFACT)
ISO/IEC 9805	Commitment, Concurrency and Recovery protocol
ISO/IEC 9945	Portable Operating System Interface (POSIX)
ISO/IEC 10026	Distributed Transaction Processing
ISO/IEC 10027: 1990	IRDS Framework
ISO/IEC 10728: 1993	Services Interface Standard

Copies of ISO/IEC 9075:1992 - Database Language SQL are available from the British Standards Institution (BSI) Publications, Linford Wood, Milton Keynes, MK14 6LE. Tel: 0908 221166.

NIST's Validated Products List

NIST's Validated Products List is updated and published quarterly. CCTA's Procurement Management Services will hold an up to date reference copy. Alternatively copies may be obtained from the:

National Technical Information Service, US Dept. of Commerce, 5285 Port Royal Road, Springfield, VA 22151, USA.

Subscriptions: 0101 703 487 4630
Individual copies: 0101 703 487 4650

Ordering number: PB91-937300

X/Open

XPG4 CAE Specification for SQL

X/Open Company Ltd., Apex Plaza, Forbury Rd, Reading, Berkshire RG21 1AX. Tel: 0734 508311.

Bibliography

General books on SQL

A Guide to the SQL Standard, CJ Date with H Darwen, Addison-Wesley, October 1992

SQL - The Standard Handbook, SJ Cannon and GAM Otten, McGraw-Hill, October 1992

Understanding the New SQL: A Complete Guide, J Melton and A Simon, Morgan Kauffman, October 1992

Glossary

	The following terms and abbreviations are used within the text of this volume. Those terms marked with an asterisk (*) are in general use but have been assigned a particular meaning within this volume.
ANSI	American National Standards Institute
Binding style	The manner in which SQL capabilities may be invoked. SQL-92 supports three binding styles: module, embedded and direct invocation.
CAE	Common Applications Environment.
CASE	Computer Assisted Software Engineering
CCR	Commitment, Concurrency and Recovery
CDIF	CASE Data Interchange Format
Conformance clause	A clause in a standard that defines the requirements on a vendor claiming conformance to that standard.
Conformance level	A set of facilities defined in a standard that a vendor may officially claim conformance to. SQL-92 has three conformance levels: Full, Intermediate and Entry. Intermediate SQL-92 is a subset of Full SQL-92; Entry SQL-92 is a subset of Intermediate SQL-92.
Connection management	Connection management is the ability of an application operating in one environment (the SQL-client environment) to connect to and access data stored in another (the SQL-server environment).
Deprecated feature	A language capability included in and fully supported by a standard but which it is intended to remove from a future version of the standard. In the standard, the deprecated features list notifies users of capabilities which if used, may cause upward compatibility problems at some time in the future.

Direct invocation	A binding style that enables SQL statements to be invoked directly, without the use of a host language.
DTP	Distributed Transaction Processing
EDI	Electronic Data Interchange.
EDIF	Electronic Data Interchange Format. A component of PDES/STEP for the exchange of data between Computer Aided Design systems.
EDIFACT	EDI for Administration, Commerce and Transport.
Embedded binding style	A binding style where SQL statements are embedded within the host programming language statements.
Export/Import*	A proposal for an international standard for moving information into or out of an SQL database environment.
Flagger facility	A capability which identifies SQL statements that use facilities not defined in a specified conformance level of a standard.
Free text data	Data that is not of a fixed format such as natural language sentences or documents.
Free text information retrieval	Applications that search free text data.
FTAM	File Transfer, Access and Management
GMT	Greenwich Mean Time. Now renamed UTC.
Host Language	A programming language used in an SQL application to provide control flow and other operations not provided by SQL.
IEC	International Electrotechnical Commission. IEC entered into a cooperative agreement with ISO via Joint Technical Committee 1 to jointly publish information technology standards.
IGES	International Graphical Exchange Specification. Due to be replaced by PDES/STEP.

Implementation-defined	A characteristic of an SQL implementation which the standard requires to be defined, but which is not defined in the standard.
Implementation-dependent	A characteristic of an SQL implementation which the standard does not require to be defined.
IRDS	Information Resource Dictionary System.
ISAM	Index Sequential Access Method.
ISO	International Organization for Standardization.
ISO 10646	An international standard for character sets.
Migration*	The task of moving applications from an implementation of one version of the SQL standard to an implementation of another version of the SQL standard.
Module binding style	A binding style where SQL statements are not embedded within the host language. The application communicates with SQL using host language CALL statements. These CALL statements invoke SQL procedures that are contained in an SQL module. The SQL procedures contain the SQL statements to be executed. Values are passed between the application program and the SQL procedures using parameters.
MUMPS	A programming language initially developed for maintaining medical data: Massachusetts University Medical Programming System. MUMPS is expected to become an ISO standard in 1994.
National Institute of Standards & Technology	A US government agency responsible for American standards.
ODA	Open Document Architecture.
ODIF	Open Document Interchange Format.
PDES/STEP	Product Data Exchange using STEP / Standard for the Exchange of Product Model Data.
PICS	See Protocol Implementation Conformance Statement.

Platform	The hardware and software required to support development tools and applications.
Protocol Implementation Conformance Statement	A description of the underlying characteristics required for two implementations of a protocol, such as RDA, to communicate successfully.
RDA	Remote Database Access.
RPC	Remote Procedure Call
SAG	SQL-Access Group.
SDIF	SGML Document Interchange Format.
SFQL	Structured Free-text Query Language
SGML	Standard Generalised Mark-up Language.
SQL	An abbreviation for Structured Query Language (pronounced 'SEQUEL'), but a misnomer as SQL provides data access and manipulation as well as querying and does not provide the control structures which would be expected of a structured language.
SQL application	An application which makes use of SQL to access and manipulate data stored in a database.
SQL-client	That part of an SQL implementation which processes connection management SQL statements. An SQL-client processes requests from a user or application and if necessary, forwards them to an SQL-server for execution.
SQL database	Any database whose data can be accessed and manipulated by SQL, but usually a relational database.
SQL implementation	Either a product which implements the SQL language and allows the writing of SQL applications or a database which can be accessed by SQL.
SQL-server	That part of an SQL implementation which manages data and responds to requests forwarded from an SQL client.

Glossary

Standard-conforming program	A program whose SQL statements are written using only facilities defined in an SQL standard. Such programs are generally portable between standards-conforming implementations, except for problems caused by incompatible implementation-defined characteristics.
Structured Full-text Query Language	An SQL-like language developed to handle free-text.
TCP/IP	Transmission Control Protocol / Internet Protocol. Protocols for data communications networks.
TP Context	Transaction Processing Context.
Transition Period*	The period between when a standard becomes superseded by a new standard and when implementations of the new standard become available.
UTC	Universal coordinated time; formerly called Greenwich Mean Time.
Vendor*	An organisation responsible for the implementation and selling of database software.
VPL	Validated Products List.
X/Open	An international public limited company promoting vendor and user interests in the area of open systems.
XPG	The brand mark associated with a vendor's product which conforms to a particular version of the X/Open CAE specifications (formerly the X/Open Portability Guides). The CAE specifications are currently on their fourth iteration, hence XPG4.

Index

Applicability of SQL	15
Application portability	50
Benefits of open systems	13
Benefits of SQL	16
Bibliography	75
Business approach	9
Business context of IS	9
CASE and 4GLs	21
Challenges facing IT	11
Client/server computing	21
Communications standards	30
Compatibility of Entry SQL-92 with SQL-89	71
Conformance and timescales	45
Conformance testing and vendor claims	45
Consortia standardisation bodies	42
Data integration	22
Data interchange standards	28
Data management standards	27
Entry SQL-92	61
Evolution of the standard	31
Export/import	41

FIPS/PUBS	58
Full SQL-92	67
Future development	8
Future developments of SQL	53
Glossary	79
Implementation defined limits	51
Information resource dictionary system (IRDS)	40
Intermediate SQL-92	62
International standard	57
International standard for SQL	31
Introduction	1
Introduction to SQL	9
Keywords	8, 73
Migration	72
National standards	57
New reserved keywords	73
New facilities in SQL-92	35
Object-oriented technology	24
Object database management systems	25
Overview of SQL	14
Overview: summary of key messages	5
Performance testing	51
Procurements involving RDA	52

Index

Procurements involving SQL	7, 49
Purpose of this volume	1
Related standardisation activities	39
Related technologies	21
RDA conformance testing	47
Remote database access (RDA)	39
Role of open systems	12
Scope of SQL-92	32
SQL-Access group	42
SQL conformance	7
SQL3 facilities	53
SQL, RDA and procurements	49
SQL standards process	31
SQL-supporting international standards	39
SQL-92 conformance claims and testing	46
SQL-92 conformance levels	33
Standards context of SQL	26
Structured Full-Text Query Language	44
Terminology	3
Technical context of SQL	21
Technical approach	11
Timescales for RDA	48
Timescales for SQL3	56

Database Language SQL Explained

Timescales for SQL-92   47

Transaction processing standards   29

Vendor specifications   58

X/Open   43